I0813361

FOX UNDER THE MOON

Seasons of Comfort and Hope

Stacey McNeill

weldonowen

For anyone who has ever known
the sheer joy, and utter
heartbreak, of being able to
truly feel.

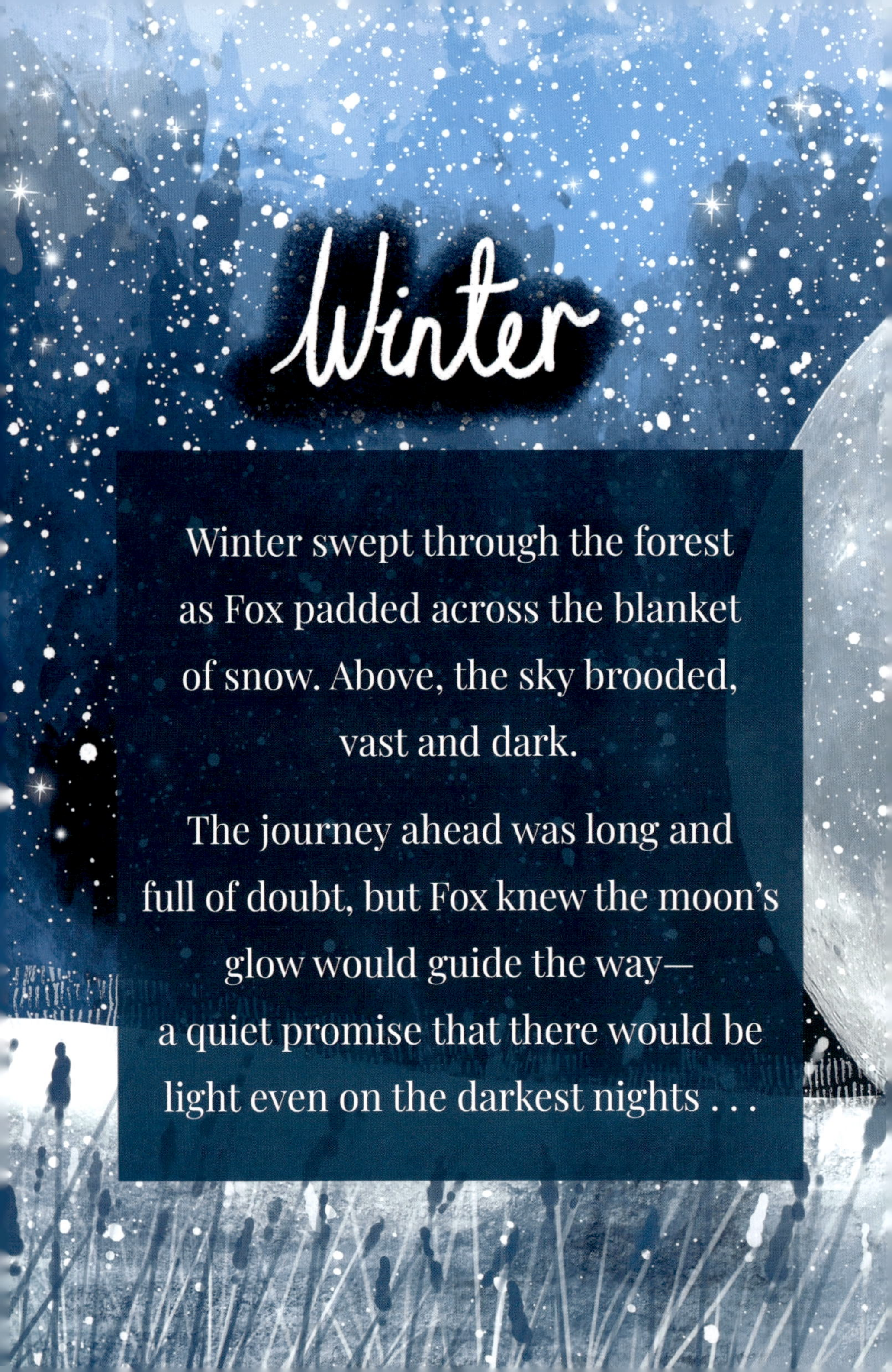

Winter

Winter swept through the forest as Fox padded across the blanket of snow. Above, the sky brooded, vast and dark.

The journey ahead was long and full of doubt, but Fox knew the moon's glow would guide the way—a quiet promise that there would be light even on the darkest nights . . .

"Why are you always out at night?" asked the fox.

"Because..."
replied the
moon,

"...it's only
in the darkness
that we can
see the stars."

"Look back and see
how far
you've come,
The mountains
you have climbed,
You'll get there when
you're meant to,
One step at
a time."

"I think I've lost
all hope,"
said the fox.

"There is always hope," replied the moon, "even if it's just the faintest glimmer, it's always there... like stars in the night sky."

"I do like stars," replied the fox.

"Sometimes it's hard to see a path through the trees," moon said,

"So take the step in front of you and see what lies ahead...

...focus on the small things, take it day by day ~

You'll see in time
those steps add up,
and you will find
your way."

"Winter nights
are cold,"
said the fox,
"but being with you
always
keeps my heart
warm."

"Things are always
better when
you're here,"
Said the fox,
"you lift me up
somehow."

"That's what friends
are for,"
replied the moon.

"In a forest
full of
magic,

And a sky
alight with
stars,

You're still the
most enchanting
thing,

I've ever seen
by far."

"I feel so small,"
said the fox.

"So do the stars,"
replied the moon,
"and yet the
night sky would be
nothing without them."

"Stars are amazing,"
said the
fox.

"And so are you,"
replied
the moon.

"I don't really like the dark," said the fox

"Hold on," replied the moon, "no winter lasts forever."

"I'm not sure I can carry on," said the fox.

"But look how far you've come already," replied the moon,

"you weren't sure you could keep going yesterday, yet look where you are today."

"It's so hard,"
said the fox.

"I know,"
replied the
moon,

"but remember,
it's the difficult
times in life

that have the
most to teach us."

"What is courage?"
asked
the fox.

"Courage is to trust and
believe in
yourself no matter
what,"
replied the
moon,

"and to know
deep down that you
can keep going...
...even
when you
feel afraid."

"Often it's
the little things,
The small gifts
from above,
That let us know
we're always close,
To the ones
we love."

"How far can love travel?" asked the fox.

"Further than you could ever imagine," replied the moon.

"To the moon and back?" asked the fox.

"At least," replied the moon.

"Sit here in the dark
with me,
Underneath the moon,

We don't have to
Say a word,

I'll just be here
with you."

"I'm afraid,"
said the fox

"But you are also brave," replied the moon, "the choice you must make is which voice you allow to speak loudest."

"It's OK to take some time..." said the moon.

"We all need
rest to feel
whole again."

"How long does
love last?"
asked the fox.

"Longer than a lifetime," replied the moon, "and for some it never fades."

"Love is an amazing thing,
It feels like coming home,
So when somebody gives it to you,
Never let it go.

When you feel another's love,
Hold on to it tight...

"...And when your world's in darkness, Love will shine a light."

"Talking helps,
doesn't it?"
asked the fox.

"Always," replied
the moon,

"and I'm always
here to listen when
you need
a friend."

"Sometimes it's
the little things,

That warm your
heart and soul,

The smallest acts
of Kindness,

That make you
feel whole."

"What makes
life so precious?"
asked the fox.

"The special moments
we get to spend
together,"
replied the moon.

"So be grateful for
each and every one."

"You're stronger than you realize,

And you've come so very far,

So when your world's
in darkness,

Make sure you
look for
stars."

"I wish
things could
just be easy,"
said
the fox.
"Life is full of
ups and downs,"
replied the moon,

"and it's through
the difficult
times
that we learn
just how
resilient
we really
are."

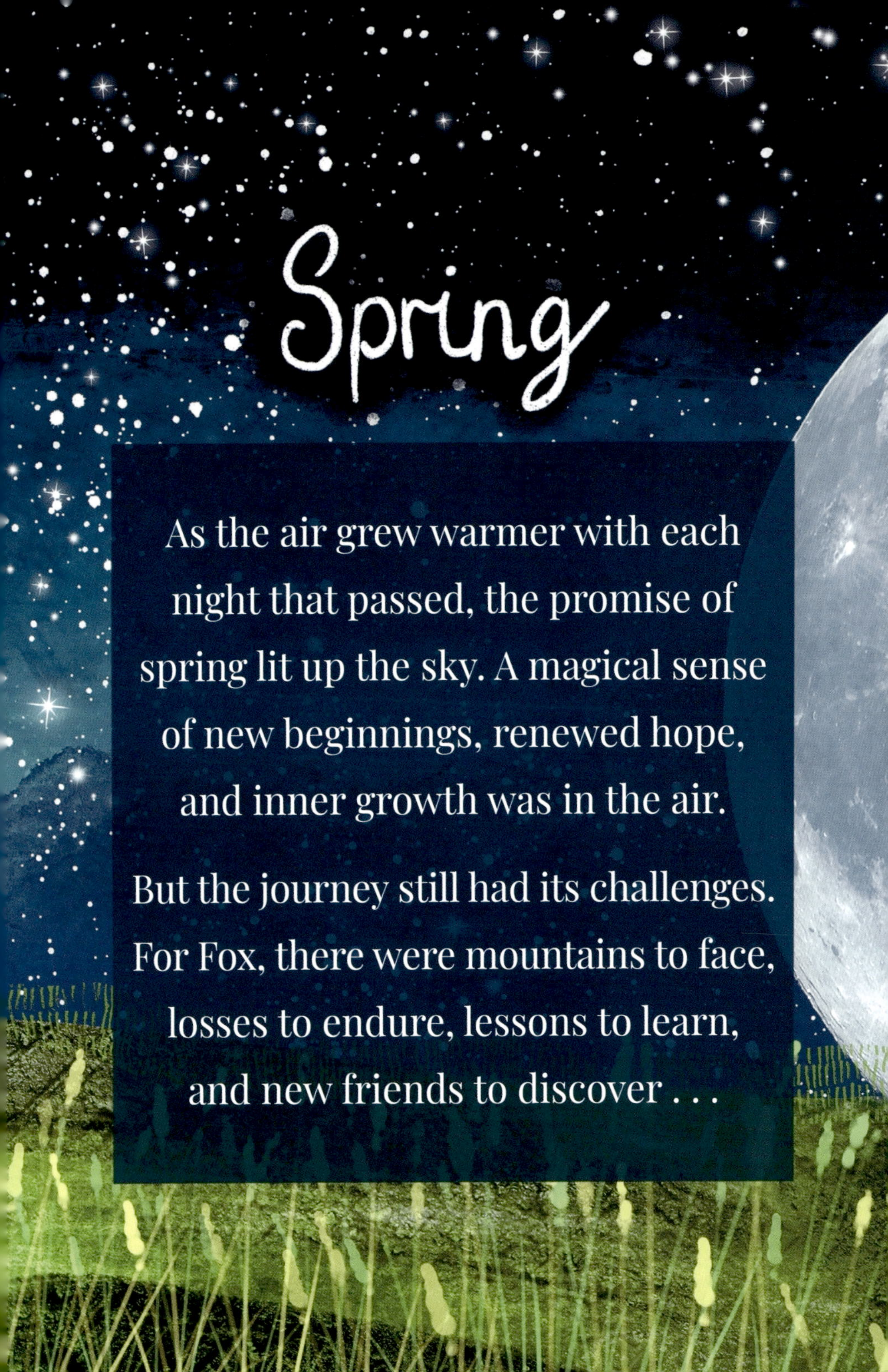

Spring

As the air grew warmer with each night that passed, the promise of spring lit up the sky. A magical sense of new beginnings, renewed hope, and inner growth was in the air.

But the journey still had its challenges. For Fox, there were mountains to face, losses to endure, lessons to learn, and new friends to discover . . .

"Spring is coming,"
whispered the moon,
"to remind us
how beautiful
new beginnings
are."

"The world
is full of
beauty,
When you take the time
to see,
And it's made even
lovelier,
When you're here
next to me."

"Friends make the world a little bit more wonderful just by being in it, don't they?" Said the fox.

"However far you travel,
Old friend,
there'll always be~

A part of me
inside your
heart,

forever yours to keep."

"There is no better time,"
said the moon,
"than time spent with those you love."

"Help" is such
a little word,
And yet it is
so brave,

Sometimes we have to
ask for it,
To feel ourselves
again.

"What if I get something wrong?" asked the fox.

"Then it will be a wonderful opportunity to learn," replied the moon.

"Can wishes
come true?"
asked the
fox.

"Hope,
wish and
wonder away,"
replied the moon,
"anything is possible
when you start
small
and dream
big."

"What is life about?"
asked the fox.

"The privilege of getting to love," replied the moon, "and being loved in return... in the end that's all that matters."

"In your lowest moments,
Take a minute to be still...
Tell yourself you'll be OK,
Because I know you will."

"Does it matter who you love?" asked the fox.

"Not one bit," replied the moon, "love is love...

... and that's
the only thing
that matters."

"I promise I'll never
forget you,"
said the fox,
"even when you're
no longer there."

"We've shared too many
happy times to forget,"
replied the moon.

"I'll keep them in my
heart forever,"
said the fox.

"That way
we'll always
be together,"
replied
the moon.

"What if I fail?"
asked the fox.
"Then the worst thing
that can happen is you
will have tried,"
replied the
moon.

"And do you know the best thing about trying?"

"What?" asked the fox.

"It's never too late to try again," replied the moon.

"It's hard
to shine
all the time,"
said the star.

"Sometimes I want to give up."
said the fox.

"But I know you are strong enough to carry on,"
replied the moon.

"So in those hard times,
just Know...
I'll never give up
on you."

"Sometimes
Something magical
Is all you need to see,
To Know that there
is hope in life,
And reason
to believe."

"I know you're there above me,
Written in the stars,

And though we can't
be together,
You're forever
in my heart.

But in this sea of
darkness,
Underneath the moon,

There aren't enough
stars in the sky
to count
The times I think
of you."

"What does love feel like?" asked the fox.

"Home," replied the moon.

"It's all going to
be OK,"
said the moon,
"... but until it is, it's
OK not to be OK
sometimes too."

"Do you believe in magic?" asked the fox.

"I believe in curiosity," replied the moon, "and that is where real magic can be found."

"We have to have
the darkness,
to appreciate the
light.
We couldn't see the
stars,"
moon said,
"without the black
of night."

"How can I make
a difference?"
asked the fox.

"Be kind to others,"
replied the moon,
"for even the
smallest acts of
kindness
make the world a
better place."

When life felt like
a challenge
Fox looked up above,
Hoping for some guidance,
Wisdom, hope and love.

The moon smiled
kindly,
And knew
just what to say.
"Be still," she whispered,
"take your time,
And you
will be OK."

"Keep going,"
Said the
moon,
"for even the longest journeys
start with one first
step."

"Will I ever get there?"

asked the fox.

"In time," replied the moon,

"but there's no hurry...

...you might just find there is even more joy in the adventures you'll have along the way."

Summer brought light, warmth, and love to the forest. The world came alive with life, and fiery skies promised new adventures, joy, and encouragement to keep going.

Fox knew there was still a way to go, and that this part of the journey would call for strength, resilience, compassion, and—above all—kindness . . .

"Quietly on the darkest nights,
The moon and stars we'll share,

For real friends know,
What matters most,
Is simply being there."

"Sometimes I worry
that others
won't love
me."
said the fox.

"Do you love
yourself?"
replied the moon,
"because that's an
important
place
to start."

"How can I love myself?" asked the fox.

"Give yourself kindness," replied the moon,

"and know that no matter what, you are enough."

"Things are tough
at the moment,"
said the fox.

"Let the waves carry you
through the
turbulent times,"
replied the moon.

"Calm seas always follow a storm."

"One day I will
be starlight,
And you will
still be
here,
But even on the
longest nights,
I will keep you
near."

"Sometimes it is
difficult to
know which way to
turn,
But listen in those
moments,
For there's often lots
to learn.
Life will give you
challenges,
Oceans you
must cross,

But the best time
to find yourself,
Is when you're feeling
lost".

"What is magic?" asked the fox.
"Sharing a moment with another who understands your soul," replied the moon.
"When you feel it... you'll know."

"Talk to yourself
with kindness,
Give yourself some
time,
Have some faith
that in the end,
Things will work out
fine."

"Where can you
find happiness?"
asked the fox.

"In the simple things..."
replied the moon,
"... like shared moments,
stories and
stars."

Two otters floated
hand in hand,
In the blue lagoon,

They counted stars
together,
Beneath a crescent moon.

They held tight to
one another,
So they wouldn't
float away,

And one said to
the other,
"I love you more
each day."

"Sometimes the smallest things can mean the most," said the moon,

"so never underestimate the power of kindness."

"Just like the stars
up in the sky,

Sparkling in
the night,

No matter how
dark it may
get,

love
will shine a light."

"What is happiness?"
asked the fox.

"To live in the
present,"
replied the
moon,

"and
enjoy
what we
already
have."

"How can we find it?" asked the fox.

"You just have to open your heart to see it," replied the moon. "Happiness will find all who look for it."

"Enjoy the little moments,
Be grateful for each day."

The moon smiled
down and whispered,
"It's going to
be OK."

"I feel like I've lost my sparkle, and I'm afraid I may never get it back again," said the fox.

"Even at your lowest point,"
replied the moon,
"you still have it in you
to shine,
and you'd be amazed
at what a little
time can do."

"Next time you feel unworthy,
Or start to have self-doubt,
Remember that real beauty
Sparkles
From the inside out."

"Don't be
afraid to
start over..."
said the moon.

"New flowers bloom
from the same
ground each
Summer~
Nature's way
of showing us
that growth is an
ongoing and
beautiful
thing."

"I think I might be
broken,"
said the fox.
"I feel like I've fallen to
pieces and I may
never mend."

"You'll feel differently
in time,"
replied the moon.
"The little pieces may not
go together in quite the
same way,

but bit by bit
you will
mend...
...and when you do,
you'll be
even stronger than
before."

"We only have a little time
Before we'll be apart,
But know that wherever you go,
I'll be there in your heart."

"I know you
can
Keep going."
Said
the
wise, old
moon.

"You're stronger than you think you are, and I believe in you."

"The stars are there
to show us,"
said the moon,
"that there is hope...

"...even in darkness."

"I'm not sure
where I'm going,"
said the fox.

"Perhaps that's not such
a bad thing,"
replied the moon.
"There is calm to be
found in just letting
things be... and a
certain adventure
in allowing life
to surprise
you."

"We're not supposed to be friends,"
Said the fox.
"You can't choose who you love,"
replied the moon,

"and sometimes
the most unlikely
friendships
are
the
best."

"Why do goodbyes hurt so much?" asked the fox.

"Because they remind us how wonderful something was," replied the moon.

"even if we
didn't realize it
at the time."

The season of change blew through the forest—a cool and restless anxiousness swept in by the wind.

When everything felt as if it were falling apart, the friends struggled to move forward. But, in the glimmering hope of the starlight, and with the wise moon by their sides, they would soon discover the beauty in letting go . . .

"Sometimes I feel that
my problems aren't as
big or important as
everyone else's"
said the fox.

"Well..." replied the moon, "do they matter to you?"

"Yes," replied the fox, "very much."

"Then they are valid," replied the moon, "and guess what?"

"What?" asked the fox.

"They matter to me too," said the moon, "and so do you."

"Can I ask you
something?"
the rabbit asked
the moon above.

"Where does all
the love go,
When you lose someone
you love?"

The moon replied to rabbit,
"Even when you are
apart,
Love can never disappear,
It stays there
in your heart."

"What do you do
when things are
tough?"
asked the fox.

"I remember that
hard times pass,"
replied the moon.
"Life, like nature,
is always moving forward,
and nothing ~ good or
bad, lasts
forever."

Hang in there -
the clouds
will pass,

And in time you'll
see...

The hard times made you Stronger Than you ever thought you'd be.

"I never seem to get there," said the fox. "Things are always going wrong."

"Each and every experience in life shapes us..." replied the moon,

"...just look at the trees~ each autumn they lose everything, yet springtime gives them a chance to try again."

" The wonderful thing
with love
Is for as long as you
shall live,

There's always more
to feel,
Always more to give ~

Love will
last a lifetime,

It's so very strong,

It will always be there,
The place where you belong."

"I'll miss you
when you've gone,"
said the fox.

"I know,"
replied the
moon,
"but the love
we shared will
always remain...

...and I'll be walking
beside you on
the darkest nights
of all,
even when you can't
see me."

"It hurts so much to
miss someone,"
said the fox.

"Remember," replied the moon, "distance means so little, when you love someone so much."

"You are just as
worthy
As any other in
the world,
So don't allow
your inner voice
To stop you being
heard."

You may feel
overwhelmed
Sometimes,
And want
to run
away,

But Know that you
are capable,
Of getting through
each day.

So when things
feel scary,

And you
can't see
your way through,

Know that you're enough
and loved,
for simply being you.

"What is
grief?"
fox pondered,
and the moon
replied, "my friend...

...grief is
what our love
becomes,
when life comes
to an end."

The moon was
wise and gentle,
and whispered
from above:
"The weight of loss
we carry is
the price we
pay for love."

"There is a sort of magic that happens when you believe in yourself..." said the moon,

"... all of a sudden,
things fall
right into
place."

"I don't want to
let go,"
said the fox.

"Letting go
doesn't have to
mean forgetting,"
replied the moon,
"but it can mean the
start of a beautiful
new beginning."

"When your world's
in darkness,

And you can't
See your way
through,

Know that there's
a star above.

Shining just for you".

"I'm finding it difficult to move on," said the fox.

"Be patient with yourself," replied the moon. "Healing comes with time, and you will find peace in acceptance."

"Will I ever feel myself again?" asked the fox.

"Hard times change you, but you'll be stronger." replied the moon.

"Often we don't realize the weight of what we carry, until we are finally able to let it go."

"Being together,"
said
the moon,
"is all that
really matters."

"Little changes
add up,"
said the moon,
"so be proud of
yourself
for every step...
... no matter how
small it
may seem."

"It's hard to find
my way through
the night,"
said the fox.

"Just because you
can't see the way
ahead,
doesn't always
mean you're on the
wrong path..."
replied the moon.

"Sometimes
we have
to trust
ourselves
to walk through darkness,
before we are able
to see
the
light."

"Can you choose to be happy?"
asked the fox.

"I believe you can,"
replied the moon.

"What makes you so sure?"
asked the fox.

"Because even when they've fallen from the trees..."
replied the moon,

... autumn leaves still
choose to dance
in the
wind."

"My thoughts are being unkind to me," said the fox.

"Then you must be twice as nice to yourself," replied the moon,

"because the way you talk to yourself matters the most."

"What should I say?" asked the fox.

"That you are enough, you are important and that you are worthy of love," replied the moon. "Say all the things you would say to your dearest friend."

"That's you," said the fox.

"Everything is falling apart," said the fox.

"Or perhaps..." replied the moon,

"... it's all falling right into place."

"When there's
darkness all
around you,
And the stars don't
seem that bright,

Know that shining
deep within,
Is your own kind
of light."

"I feel stuck,"
said the fox.

"Believe in the timing of life..." replied the moon.

"We often find the most wonderful things in the places we least expect them, and at the times we need them most."

"Goodbye," said the fox.

"For now," replied the moon.

"Is this the end?" asked the fox.

"No..." replied the moon, "...it's just the beginning."

Acknowledgments

To my dear family and friends—thank you for being my unwavering supporters, my endless sources of laughter, and my greatest encouragers. This book exists because of you, your love, your belief in me, and the magic you so freely share.

You remind me, often without even trying, of the goodness that lies within and around me, and of the power of believing—believing in myself, in each other, and in the beauty of having faith in what is yet to come.

To those whose love and inspiration spans across miles, and yet feels as close as a heartbeat—I carry you with me always, and out of sight is never out of mind.

To Adrian and Kate Herring—you know what you have done for us both personally and professionally, but you may never quite understand the value and impact your kindness has had.

A special thank-you to my incredible husband, Jamie, who holds tightly to my ankles when my head is in the sky, grounding me when I need it most, but giving me the freedom to soar. Your love and patience are the anchors that keep me steady, and the adventures we share together are my greatest inspiration.

Huge thanks to my wonderful editor, Kate Hewson, for having the vision and belief in Fox Under The Moon®, and to the wider team at Quercus Books and Hachette UK for helping to bring to life the little pieces of magic on every page.

Finally, I want to say an enormous thank-you to my army of readers and social media followers—I count you all as friends, and without the community we have built, this would all still be a distant dream. With all my heart, I am deeply grateful for this wild and exciting journey; and for the beautiful souls I get to share it with.

About the Author

Stacey McNeill is a British author whose heartwarming words and pictures have captured the imaginations of readers of all ages. In 2023, her series of uplifting picture books for adults won the prestigious Gift of the Year People's Choice Award, a testament to the joy and encouragement her work brings to so many.

Stacey founded her brand, Fox Under the Moon®, with humble beginnings—from a tiny touring caravan in North Wales to a vibrant online community with over a quarter of a million followers worldwide.

Her whimsical illustrations and sensitive words have a special way of making everyday moments feel magical, reminding her audience that a little bit of encouragement and love can go a long way. Stacey's work continues to inspire those seeking positivity, comfort, and a reminder that there is always light to be found, even on the darkest of nights.

Inspired by wildlife, woodlands, and magical night skies, Stacey now lives with her husband, Jamie, in the North East of England; and the pair run Fox Under The Moon® together, with the intention of helping others find beautiful ways to say the things that really matter.

More about Stacey can be found at www.foxunderthemoonart.com and by searching for Fox Under The Moon on social media.

First published in Great Britain in 2025 by Quercus, a Hachette UK company

First published in the United States in 2026 by Weldon Owen

weldon**owen**
an imprint of Insight Editions
P.O. Box 3088
San Rafael, CA 94912
www.weldonowen.com

ISBN: 979-888674-374-6
ISBN (Signed Edition): 979-8-88674-418-7

Manufactured in China by Insight Editions

10 9 8 7 6 5 4 3 2

Until we
meet
again...